Animal Magic

7 Magical Solos for Elementary Pianists
Dennis Alexander

The world of animals can open up so many creative avenues from both composing and performing perspectives. These elementary level solos are designed to explore the sights, sounds and characters of several interesting animals through imaginative and artistic compositions that encompass a wide range of the instrument, yet never require a stretch beyond a five-finger position. Students will discover a colorful mixture of melody and harmony and will also be delighted by some of the optional duet parts, which can be played by the teacher, parent or another student. From "Gnu Sounds" to "Woodpecker Blues," students are going to have lots of fun performing every piece from this collection! Enjoy.

Dennis Alexander

Alfred

Music engraving: Nancy Butler
Illustration: Liana Kelley • Cover design: Candace Smith

There's a Hippo in My Tree!

Dennis Alexander

Optional Duet Accompaniment (Student plays one octave higher.)

Woodpecker Blues

Dennis Alexander

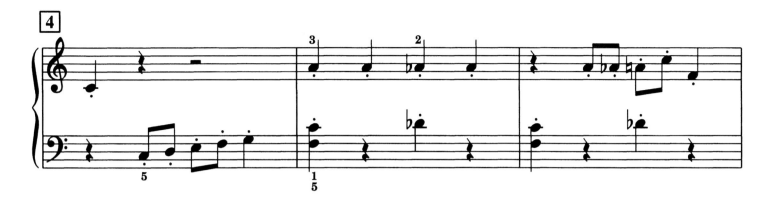

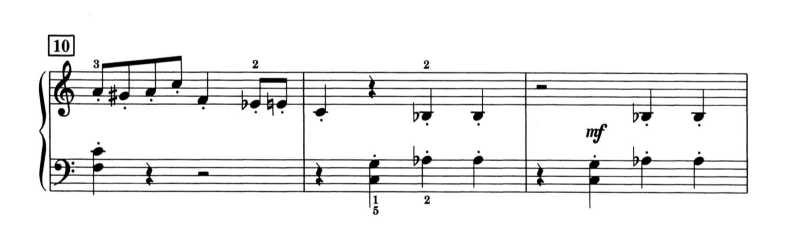

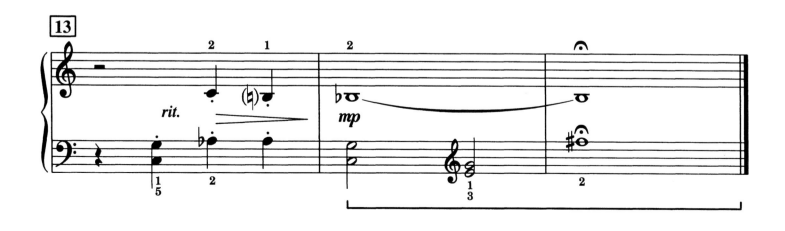

The Cantankerous Kangaroo

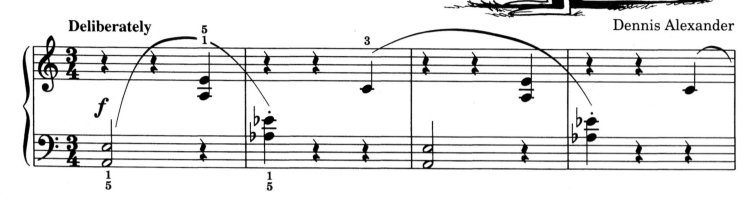

Dennis Alexander

Deliberately

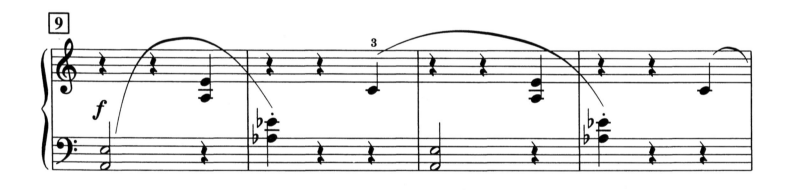

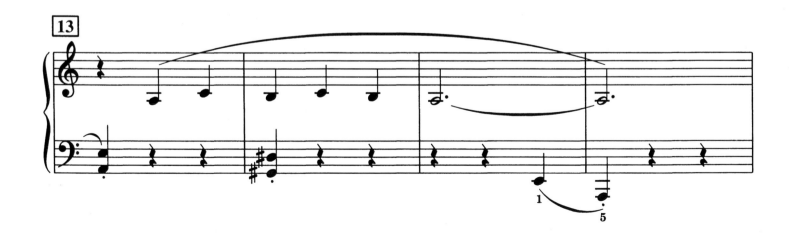

A Hairy Canary Named Fred

Cantabile

Dennis Alexander

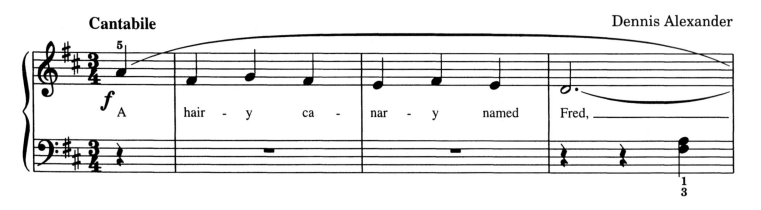

f A hair - y ca - nar - y named Fred, _____

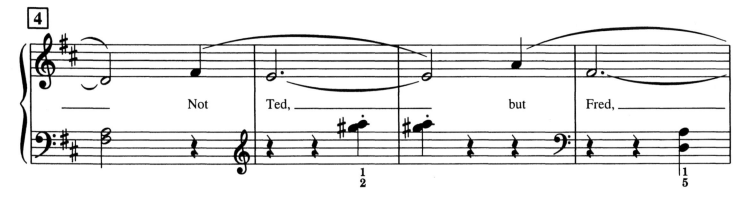

_____ Not Ted, _____ but Fred, _____

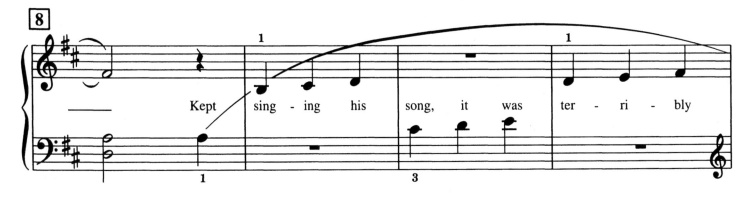

_____ Kept sing - ing his song, it was ter - ri - bly

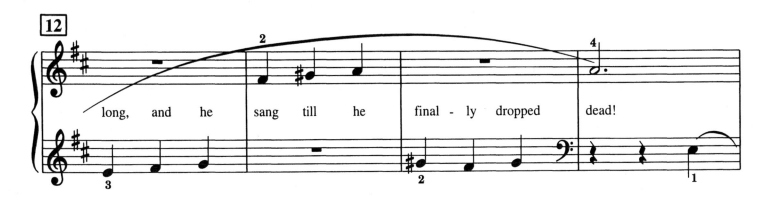

long, and he sang till he final - ly dropped dead!

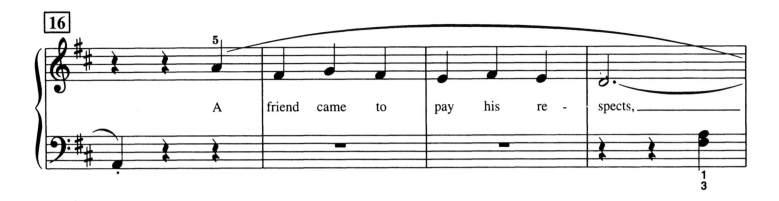

A friend came to pay his re- spects, _____

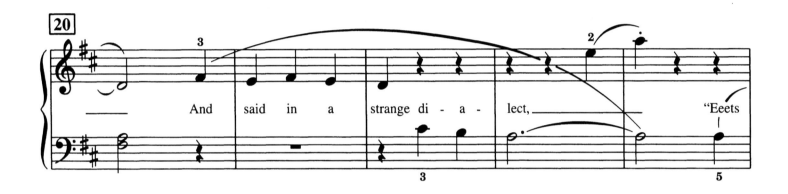

_____ And said in a strange di - a - lect, _____ "Eeets

now plain to see, Fred ees pure hees - to - ree, but his

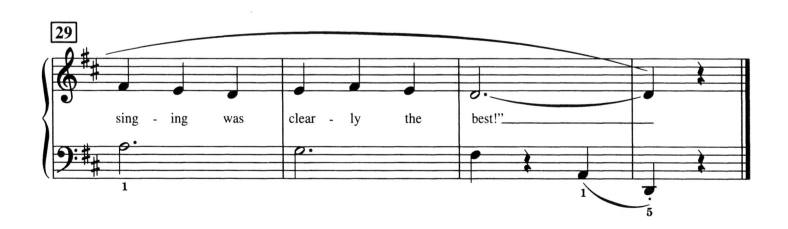

sing - ing was clear - ly the best!" _____

Slippery, Slimery, Slithery Snake

Creepily

Dennis Alexander

sempre legato

Slip - per - y, Sli - mer - y, Slith - er - y Snake, he is

creep - ing a - long, all the day long.

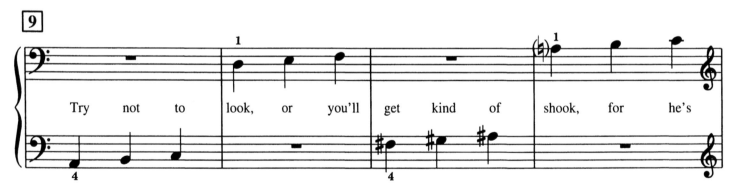

Try not to look, or you'll get kind of shook, for he's

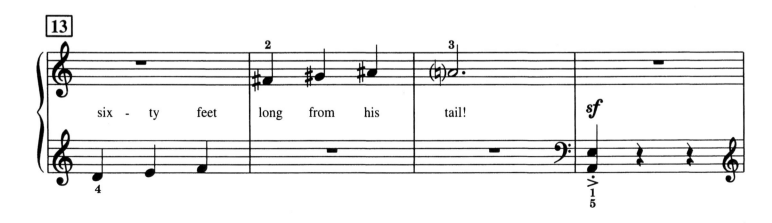

six - ty feet long from his tail!

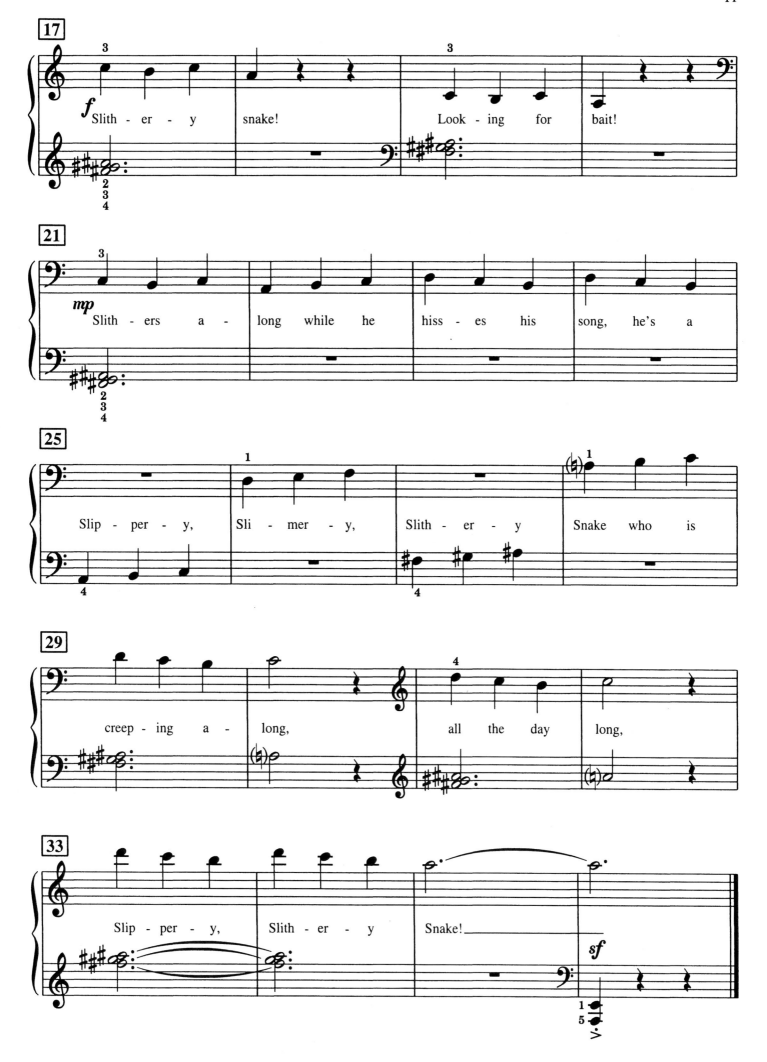

No Non-Scents!

Allegretto

Dennis Alexander

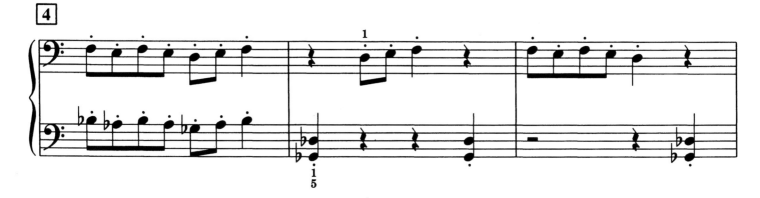

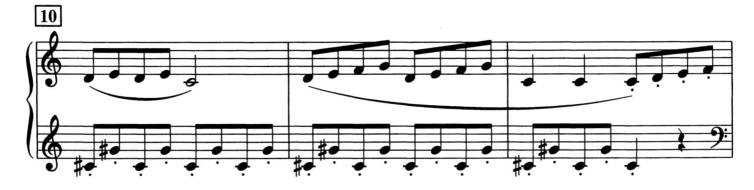

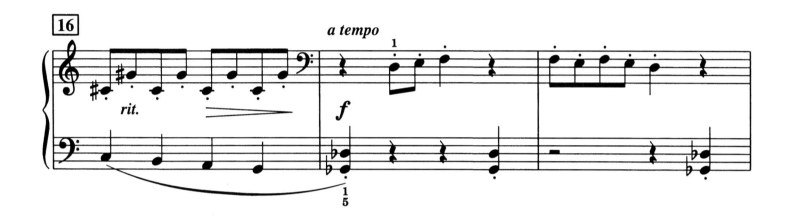

Gnu Sounds

According to ancient folklore, the Gnu is said to have been created from all the left-over parts of other animals! It looks something like a cross between a buffalo and a cow, and when it runs, it often looks as though it is going in all directions at once.

Playfully

Dennis Alexander

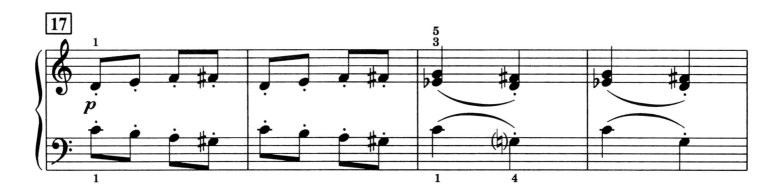

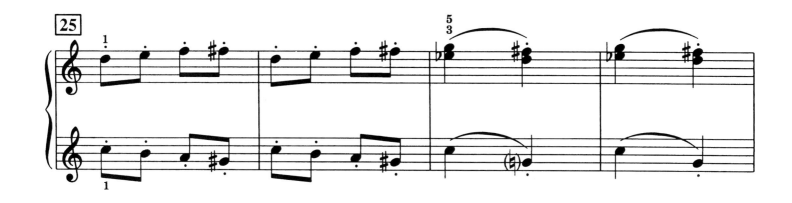

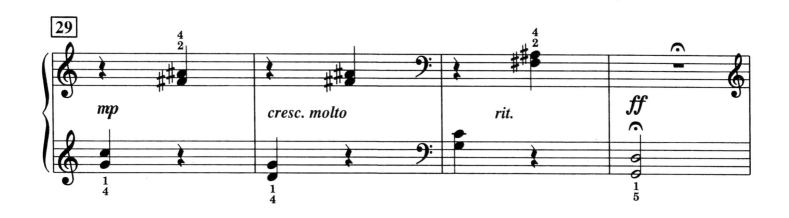

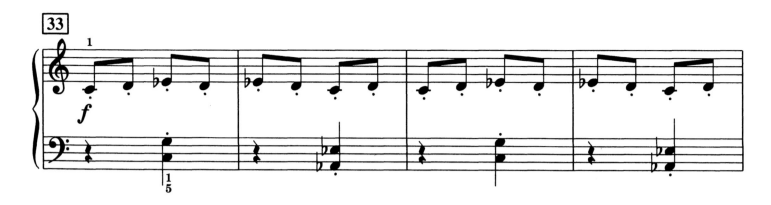

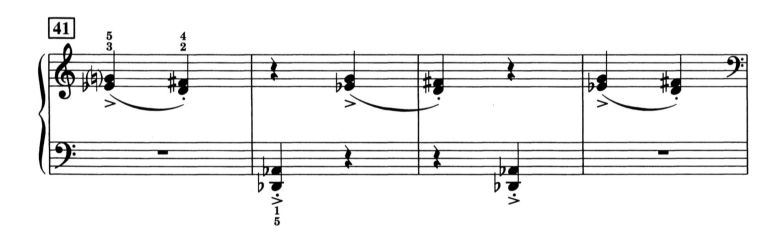

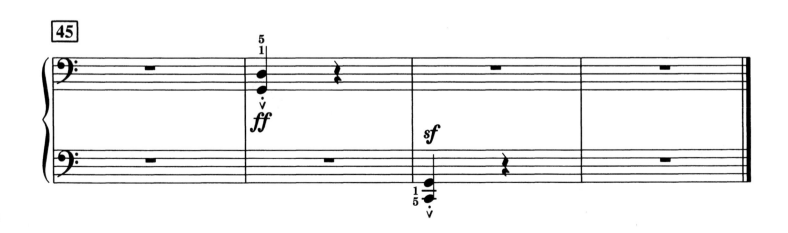